Dogs that Help

Written by Helen Dineen

Collins

Clever dogs can assist by alerting us and helping with jobs.

Alerting

Dogs are paired with the right partner. Pepper is a seeing dog.

Her partner cannot see well.
Pepper alerts him to stop at the kerb.

Stella is a hearing dog.

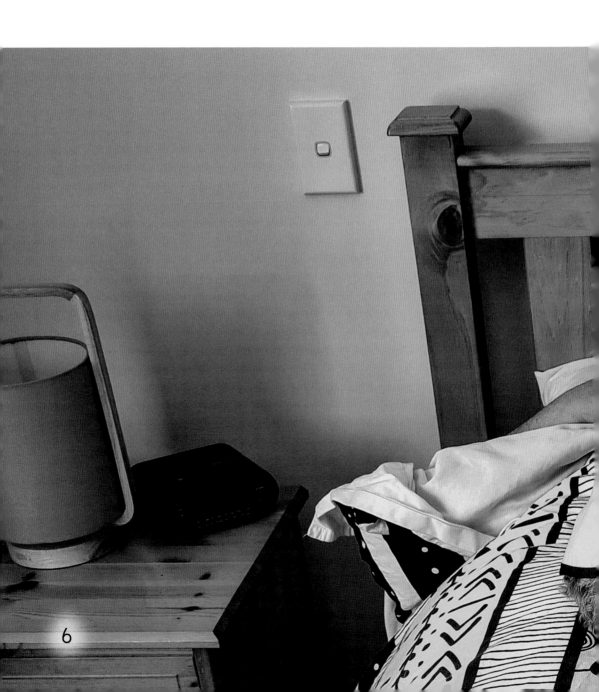

When the alarm beeps, she alerts her partner with a tap.

Helping

Support dogs help partners by picking things up.

They grip and pull to get milk and food too.

Winston helps children feel better by hugging them when they feel stressed.

Pumpkin has a strong bond with Brandon.